POSTMODERN ENCOUNTERS

Wittgenstein and Psychoanalysis

John M. Heaton

Series editor: Richard Appignanesi

ICON BOOKS UK

TOTEM BOOKS USA

Published in the UK in 2000
by Icon Books Ltd., Grange Road,
Duxford, Cambridge CB2 4QF
email: info@iconbooks.co.uk
www.iconbooks.co.uk

Published in the USA in 2000
by Totem Books
Inquiries to: PO Box 223,
Canal Street Station,
New York, NY 10013

Distributed in the UK, Europe,
Canada, South Africa and Asia
by the Penguin Group:
Penguin Books Ltd.,
27 Wrights Lane,
London W8 5TZ

In the United States,
distributed to the trade by
National Book Network Inc.,
4720 Boston Way, Lanham,
Maryland 20706

Published in Australia in 2000
by Allen & Unwin Pty. Ltd.,
PO Box 8500, 9 Atchison Street,
St. Leonards, NSW 2065

Library of Congress catalog
card number applied for

Text copyright © 2000 John M. Heaton

The author has asserted his moral rights.

Series editor: Richard Appignanesi

No part of this book may be reproduced in any form, or by any
means, without prior permission in writing from the publisher.

ISBN 1 84046 132 2

Typesetting by Wayzgoose

Printed and bound in the UK by
Cox & Wyman Ltd., Reading

What is the price of Experience? Do men buy it
for a song?
Or wisdom for a dance in the street? No, it is
bought with the price
Of all that a man hath, his house, his wife, his
children,
Wisdom is sold in the desolate market where none
come to buy,
And in the wither'd field where the farmer plows
for bread in vain.

William Blake, 'Vala: Night the Second'

Lies nicht mehr – schau!
Schau nicht mehr – geh!
[Do not read any more – look!
Do not look any more – go!]

Paul Celan, 'Engführung'

Sigmund Freud (1856–1939) and Ludwig Wittgenstein (1889–1951) were both Viennese: Freud lived most of his life there but died in London; Wittgenstein was brought up in Vienna but spent many years in England, teaching at Cambridge where he died.

Freud created psychoanalysis and Wittgenstein is perhaps the greatest 20th-century philosopher.

3

Wittgenstein was familiar with Freud's early work – especially the *Interpretation of Dreams* and his *Jokes and their Relation to the Unconscious* – and often quoted from them. Indeed, Wittgenstein's sister had a short analysis with Freud and was mainly responsible for helping him escape from the Nazis. Living in Vienna in the 1920s enabled Wittgenstein to be familiar with the practice of analysis. Friends and relations looked to it as a way out of their personal problems.

Wittgenstein was influenced by Freud's work and thought his own work was a therapy too. He was greatly impressed – although critical – when he first read Freud, and wrote:

Unless you think very clearly psycho-analysis is a dangerous & foul practice, & it's done no end of harm &, comparatively, very little good.[1]

Wittgenstein's therapy and its relation to psychoanalysis will be the theme of this book.

Illusion

Both Freud and Wittgenstein were centrally concerned with illusion and the harm it does. Freud was a physician and approached his work as an empirical scientist. People came to him with their troubles expecting him to cure them. Acting like a physician, he 'discovered' the unconscious as the cause of illusion, classified his patients according to their type of unconscious conflict – neurosis, psychosis, perversion, hysteria and so on – and developed a technique of cure with its technical vocabulary (which included words like id, super-ego, projection and transference). He also founded a school with training courses, and criteria for entry and exit, to further the technique he had created.

Wittgenstein, on the other hand, worked within the philosophical tradition of therapy, which includes Socrates and Hellenistic philosophers such as the Epicurians, Sceptics and Stoics. More modern philosophers such as Spinoza, Hegel and Marx were all concerned with illusion and the unhappiness it brings.

Wittgenstein saw that we are prisoners of the delusive power of language. This brought him close to literature as well as philosophy. The shamming power of the word can simulate real things so well that no discriminating power of the word allows us to distinguish lies from truth. It can deceive us in the very act of singling us out as those to whom truth is delivered.

He struggled to get a clear view of what troubles us. Deep-seated ways of thinking and speaking have a hold on us. These are not single items but part of our whole style of thinking and expressing ourselves. Thus our obsession with finding answers, solutions and cures to our difficulties affects the kind of attention we give ourselves and is itself a source of illusion. We elevate certain kinds of discourse, especially scientific and medical, and make them the paradigm for the solution of all difficulties. But smugness, greed, stupidity and ambition are not psychiatric disorders; they are illusions that dominate a world vowed to self-seeking ends.

Wittgenstein did not develop a technical vocabulary and did not claim to treat a particular group of people, nor was he interested in founding a school – for all these activities can lead to further illusion.

The sickness of a time is cured by an alteration in the mode of life of human beings, and it was possible for the sickness of philosophical problems to get cured only through a changed mode of thought and of life, not through a medicine invented by an individual.[2]

Teaching

Wittgenstein wrote and taught in a very different way from Freud and most psychoanalysts. The way they taught throws light on their notion of therapy.

I must be nothing more than the mirror in which my reader sees his own thinking with all its deformities & with this assistance can set it in order.[3]

Wittgenstein thought that simply being told a truth is useless as long as error stands in its place. We must find the *path* from error to truth and for that we must plunge into the water of doubt again and again.

*One **cannot** speak the truth; – if one has not yet conquered oneself. One **cannot** speak it – but not, because one is still not clever enough. The truth can be spoken only by someone who is already **at home** in it; not by someone who still lives in untruthfulness, & does no more than reach out towards it from within untruthfulness.*[4]

He was not adding to knowledge or correcting mistakes: lecturing, giving information, and writing treatises is a suitable way for doing that. The confusions he was concerned with were due to bewitchment, fascination and illusion. They required a change of attitude, a resignation of feeling rather than of intellect, thoughtfulness rather than cleverness. He wrote and taught accordingly.

We cannot force thought but a disruption needs to happen before we can become thoughtful. The admonition to think harder may produce fidgets and frowns but it will not produce thought, as thought cannot be produced. Thinking is not a production line. Compulsive 'thinking', usually experienced as being in the head and which is far from clear, is not thoughtfulness.

No one can think a thought for me in the way no one can don my hat for me.[5]

For the last 20 or so years of his life, Wittgenstein wrote philosophical *remarks*. He found that his thoughts were crippled if he tried to force them in a specific direction against their natural inclination and that *that* was connected with the very nature of his investigations. Significantly, he often left big spaces between the remarks, so avoiding a continuous prose style. He uses no chapter headings or tables of content. He does not report or write up results. His remarks make one travel over a wide field of thought, criss-crossing in every direction and often approaching the same point from different directions. This gives an *übersicht* (survey, overview) of the problem and stops us being fixed on one way of looking at it. He uses no technical vocabulary and is explicitly aware that any philosophical assertion he makes has an imprecise and dubious status. His remarks are hints to be applied to confusions and are not dazzling novelties of technical insight. He rejects certainty as a standard of truth in favour of exactness of insight.

*I believe I summed up where I stand in relation to philosophy when I said: really one should write philosophy only as one **writes a poem**.*[6]

He was a master of the German language and a great stylist. His written style was direct and simple with no purple patches, but lively because of its variation in pace, length and balance of the sentences and the wealth of apt examples. It invites direct involvement in the text by the reader because it is a drama of self-interrogation inviting the recognition of wishes, temptations and entanglements rather than arguments for the passive acceptance of theses.

Writing the right style means setting the carriage precisely on the rails.[7]

He taught in the same way; he did not lecture. Students would sit in a circle with him and he would think before the class in a visible struggle with his thoughts. He often felt confused and said so. The meetings were commonly conversational, and he would try to draw a thought out of himself and help others to do the same. There were frequent and prolonged silences in an atmosphere of the stillest attention and extreme seriousness – an atmosphere likely to wrench one out of one's usual thoughtless banalities, but holding the risk that it can be imitated by fanatics.

He did not force people to express themselves. This leads to pointless talk, insane quantities of words and images that drown thought. It can be a relief to have nothing to say, because only then there may be a chance to be thoughtful. And sometimes there is no point in saying anything. The notions of relevance, necessity, the point of something, are of much greater significance than the outpouring of knowledge and explanations. His aims were the deeply practical ones of teaching a skill by means of examples and preventing understanding that is unaccompanied by a change in one's way of life.

The philosopher strives to find the liberating word, that is, the word that finally permits us to grasp what up until now has intangibly weighed down our consciousness.[8]

The writing and teaching of most psychoanalysts, on the other hand, invite one to enter a world of secure moorings. They are reports of facts, meanings, interpretations, and theories that they or their master have discovered – a dominant and endless discourse that soothes and keeps us in line. Freud was a masterful lecturer. In his *Introductory Lectures on Psychoanalysis*,[9] he tells us unfalteringly of his discoveries, just as if he were a physicist lecturing to undergraduates on his discoveries on the nature of matter. His knowledge, he claims, is based on innumerable observations and experiences by himself and his colleagues, and it can be confirmed by going into psychoanalysis ourselves, just as a physicist's knowledge can be confirmed by experiment.

Freud thought for people. He gave them knowledge of the content of their minds, never questioning the nature of this knowledge. He assumed his colleagues were a uniform body of people free of illusion, who had discovered in their minds more or less what he had found in his.

He took little notice of the duplicitous and scheming nature of mind which stretches far beyond neurosis. Supposing some of his colleagues were smug, would they be free of illusion?

As time went by, psychoanalysts came up with different accounts of the nature of the mind and explanations of the causes of neurosis. Each account has its believers, and there have been numerous splits and schools each tending to claim its origins from Freud. The main constant, however, is belief in the unconscious.

We are rarely invited to make our own judgements about our minds and take responsibility for them. Instead, we are expected to stand on the shoulders of the teacher, a stance appropriate in learning a science but useless in therapy where we need a particular quality of attention and to take responsibility for what we are doing. Therapy to Wittgenstein is a thinking shared by two in which the courage to be foolish and ignorant is more important than cleverness. He makes his struggle with language visible and in this way helps us come upon our own movement of thought.

In his search he frequently refers to his own intuitions, taste, feelings and temptations: 'It seems to me . . . ', 'I've a feeling that . . . ', 'Something tells me . . . ', 'Now we want to . . . ', 'Here the urge is strong . . . ', are frequent expressions of his. There are questions, jokes, reminders, parables and striking absurd examples.

Don't for heaven's sake, be afraid of talking nonsense! Only don't fail to pay attention to your nonsense.[10]

He makes room for wit. He appreciated Freud's wit: his ability to make witty comparisons between money and shit, obsessional rituals and some religious practices, mutilation and castration; his wit in asserting that we resist psychoanalytic truth because of our sexual inhibitions (a sure way of getting us hastily to agree with him!); his persuasive style of writing, while at the same time asserting that he seeks not to persuade but to speak the truth.

Free Association
However, there is another side to psychoanalysis additional to its 'discoveries', theories and schools; there is its *practice*, and it is here that there are deep affinities between Freud and Wittgenstein.

Free association is the fundamental rule of psycho-analysis. This involves allowing what comes to mind to be spoken, selecting nothing and omitting nothing, and giving up any critical attitude or direct forcing in the face of a problem. The analyst, in turn, must adopt a complementary stance of 'evenly suspended attention' – that is, surrender his or her attention to the situation at hand. The fundamental rule applies, more or less, in both directions.

When we free associate we let whatever comes to mind be said. This 'whatever' is not to be taken as a statement of knowledge. The analyst does not check whether it is true or not. It opens a field of possibilities of *sense* rather than truth and falsity. Nor is it the ineffableness of the individual, but it is such as it is, singular, not having this or that property that would identify it as belonging to a class or set. The analyst is indifferent with respect to its properties.

Free association is akin to dreaming, for dreams are communicated through reports to which normal accounts of assertoric truth and falsity do not apply. We cannot point directly to the content of an occurring dream. What is reported is typically accepted, for there is no independent check. It is generally senseless to say to a person that they did not dream what they reported, although free association may alter the dream. As dreams are often apparently nonsensical, they can force upon us the question as to how language represents and makes sense – both questions of central interest to Freud and Wittgenstein. However, they differed in how they understood this.

Freud wanted to construct a science of the mind comparable to physics. He believed that all mental activity is determined and that free association leads to a repressed wish that lies in the unconscious causing the associations to dry up; thus he could infer the cause of the block in the associations. The job of the practising analyst was to observe this process and interpret the wish blocking the associations. This wish was assumed to lie at a deeper and more real level – 'in' the unconscious – than the actual associations. Free association was a means to the end of finding causes in the unconscious.

Always come down from the barren heights of cleverness into the green valleys of folly.[11]

Wittgenstein, on the other hand, wanted to resolve unclarity rather than create theories and find causes. We are like flies who have got stuck in a bottle and buzz around senselessly. We must attend carefully to how we got in. The compulsion to theorise keeps us in the bottle. We have to re-find the horizons of understanding and feeling that are implicit in our use of language, and that are forgotten when we become confused and develop symptoms. The confusions disappear and the bottle fades away when we can orient ourselves to the relevant horizon and start talking sense.

It is sense and nonsense that are important here rather than the truth of a theory. When we talk nonsense we fail to give sense to an expression but believe, often compulsively, that we are meaning something. This type of nonsense is very different from the nonsense of, for example, Lewis Carroll, Edward Lear or James Joyce in *Finnegans Wake*, where these writers are exploring the paradoxes of the absurd, the limits of sense. Wittgenstein often does this – for example: 'If a lion could talk, we could not understand him.'[12]

If in life we are surrounded by death, so too in the health of our understanding by madness.[13]

The failure of sense that requires therapy is empty, a cliché; we fall into banalities lacking thoughtfulness. Wittgenstein sought to educate our ear for nonsense, to hear the play of sound and sense, and so revitalise language by showing its rootedness in the practices of a people – how the similes and images embedded in our language can easily deceive us.

We give birth to problems because we are unaware of the manner in which our thinking and use of language creates problems. We want to achieve a desired state and go straight for it, and this then becomes a problem. Instead of being aware of how the conflicts and contradictions created by confusions in the use of language create problems and despair, we try to force them into a particular pattern to achieve a desired result, to capture one kind of experience and avoid another.

It is essential to find not merely what is to be said before a difficulty but *how* one must speak about it – hence Wittgenstein's use of philosophical remarks which are so like free associations. How something is said determines what is said – it shows the thought. Free association encourages one to focus on the activity of speaking, the way we use words, our feeling for them. The tone and gestures of our words reveal more than they can say.

Let the use of words teach you their meaning.[14]

In free associating, a game of language is being played which shows language in use, but not being used for any particular purpose. The measure of its success is that all players can move on in their own way.

Its difficulty is that we cannot easily allow free association to take place, for, ordinarily, when faced with a problem, we feel compelled to reach our goal by the shortest route, which we imagine is a straight line, so we suppress free association.

*Tell me **how** you are searching and I will tell you* *what you are searching for.*[15]

The search metaphor is one of the oldest expressions used to talk about problem-solving. We search through a problem 'space' and insight is our reward for perseverance. The search metaphor has many of the attributes of searching in physical space so it is pictured as occurring in a conceptual space or a mental one – one searches in one's mind! Then speculations are made as to what goes on in this private space of the mind. Free association frees us from the search metaphor. In the course of free associating we may remember, imagine, notice, consider, search, repeat senseless thoughts and activities, and much else. It is a struggle in language and not between processes in our minds.

There is no fixed method of free associating. It is a way of giving free rein and attention to the way our minds create meanings and make associations, bringing them together and dividing them in all sorts of ways. It helps to decentre our fixed identity that constitutes whom we believe we are. It is a struggle with oneself and the analyst in which there is no external witness, plaintiff and judge. Like psychoanalysis, it is a talking cure; but unlike psychoanalysis, there is no external authority, no ideal, to which it must correspond. The weight is put on the use of words, because this shows our approach to the problem, and it is this *showing* that lets us see the deformities that distort our thought.

*In philosophizing we may not **terminate** a disease of thought. It must run its natural course, and **slow** cure is all important.*[16]

In the course of his 'long and involved journeyings' around the subjects that concerned him, Wittgenstein made clarifying remarks designed to make us look at some phenomena in a different light. These included reminders, descriptions, jokes, metaphors and ironical comments. He clarified confusions by refraining from explanations, but showed us analogies and disanalogies revealing how we have created unities and false idols. He sought clarity of understanding through language.

Psychoanalysts often do much the same in practice, but in theory and when not in contact with actual patients, they favour formulae, causal laws and mechanisms. Speaking of Freud, Wittgenstein wrote:

It is all excellent similes, e.g. the comparison of a dream to a rebus.[17]

The familiar experience of noticing an aspect is an important feature of Wittgenstein's therapy.

I contemplate a face, and then suddenly notice its likeness to another. I see that it has not changed; and yet I see it differently. I call this experience 'noticing an aspect'.[18]

This has an air of paradox, for we see the face in a new and different way as similar to another's, but at the same time we know the face has not changed. When we see a new aspect, it is a spontaneous response. It is not a matter of the will or an inference. It *strikes* one.

Psychoanalysts often get analysands to notice aspects, although they call it interpreting. Thus, most transference interpretations are a matter of noticing aspects. If an analysand describes certain behaviour outside a session, the analyst may point out the aspect of it that occurs in the session. For example, sado-masochistic behaviour outside a session may be shown to be going on 'secretly' in the session.

The original seduction scene of psychoanalysis is an example of how confusion may begin. If a small child witnesses a scene of sexual interaction or is submitted to gestures from adults which possess a sexual connotation that is impenetrable to him or her because they are more than an expression of love, then a gap may be created that the child cannot integrate. The child becomes impotently caught in a sexual situation which is uncanny, and a traumatic experience around which thoughts and feelings circulate. He or she can't make sense of it and can't remember it, as the memory has become repressed – or better, encrypted – and so the grammar in which it could be expressed and remembered is distorted.

The effect of a false analogy taken up into language:
it means a constant battle and uneasiness (as it were

a constant stimulus). It is as if a thing seemed to be a human being from a distance, because we don't perceive anything definite, but from close up we see that it is a tree stump. The moment we move away a little and lose sight of the explanations, one figure appears to us; if after that we look more closely, we see a different figure; now we move away again, etc., etc.[19]

These specific conflicts are dissolved by attending to what is said and done. This breaks the hold of false analogies by showing the conditions of sense. We tend to see similarity where we ought to see difference and so end up speaking nonsense. The analytic situation is a 'playground' on which these confusions of language and thought can be understood and allowed to speak their name.

*A **picture** held us captive. And we could not get outside it, for it lay in our language and language seemed to repeat it to us inexorably.*[20]

If we attend to free association and the way it reveals how we use language, then no conclusions follow. Contrary to how it is used in psychoanalysis, it does not lead to claims that the mind 'must be like this'. It is not an exploration of the mind in the way we might explore the moon, where we can describe what we find. Although free association is often spoken in the language of information, it is not used in the language game of giving information. Freud claimed to have discovered sexual motives behind most of his patients' actions. Wittgenstein could not deny that sexual images and thoughts were produced when patients free associated before Freud and members of his school. But he pointed out that there is a charm in claiming sexuality as an explanation for many activities, although this does not mean that it is a universal or fundamental cause.

There is a tendency in psychoanalysis to fetishise meaning. Thus, in dream interpretation, all the material of a dream may be recuperated for the category of meaning. Wittgenstein, on the other hand, left open the possibility of phenomena that only indicate meaning without meaning anything in particular. So a dream can show but not say; it can be contemplated and not interpreted.[21]

In free associating, the activity and the clarifications direct the activity itself. Free associating and writing are not merely ways of communicating what is in the mind to be explained by the analyst. But the activities *themselves* reveal.

I really do think with my pen, for my head often knows nothing of what my hand is writing.[22]

Wittgenstein's works are filled with little sketches and rough diagrams, for these can show better than words. He argued that language has a pictorial quality.[23] It gives rise to pictures but, on the other hand, it passes into something like music.[24] Painting, drawing and the musical arts can be ways of showing the problem and do not need interpretations from outside. Psychoanalysts rarely use them in therapy, for according to their theory only verbal interpretations are mutative. However, Winnicott's 'Squiggle Game', in which he and a child made alternate squiggles on paper that evoked significant meanings, is an example of how such activities reveal.[25]

Perspicuous Representation

One of Wittgenstein's distinctive conceptions of therapy is condensed in his notion of perspicuous representation (*übersichtliche Darstellung*). He was probably influenced in this by Breuer and Freud, who found that hysterical symptoms disappear when the patient can express the source of the trouble and acknowledge it as an appropriate expression – the crucial point being that it is the patient who acknowledges it and it is not the hypothesis of an observer seeking a cause.

Perspicuity is central to peace of mind because it brings awareness of the way we breed problems in our misuse and misunderstanding of language. In a conflict we must find the liberating word, because only when we hit upon the 'physiognomy' of the situation exactly can we move on. The physiognomy is a matter of taking the pulse of a situation, rather than taking blood, analysing it, and giving an explanation. The right human word has a physiognomy. It is 'whatever' like a face – not a universalisation nor an individuation. We need a clear view of the use of words; the manner that is neither bound by rules nor is foundational, but engenders speech. Finding the right expression does not mean accurately expressing a preconceived thought, but rather the thought this expression gives us satisfies and relieves.

A perspicuous representation is not made from the position of a disembodied spectator or a bird's eye view. It is not based on the look but on the glance or series of glances.[26] It is more like a Japanese ink painting in which everything that is marked on the surface remains visible so we are aware of its unfolding. It is from the body of labour, working through, that the animation of the expression emerges. It occurs with appropriate forms of expression and this takes time. In his notebooks, Wittgenstein tried many forms of expression before hitting the nail on the head with the right expression. People in therapy do the same. We cannot get outside the interweave of life and language. All distinctions must be drawn within it. A perspicuous representation brings about a Gestalt-switch by highlighting a new aspect of our use of words. This disperses an existing fog and resists the temptation to create theories and theoretical entities used to explain.

The inexpressible (what I find enigmatic & cannot express) perhaps provides the background, against which whatever I was able to express acquires meaning.[27]

Perspicuity is not tidiness and does not require a technical vocabulary. It means to render clear the relationships in a tangle. Simplicity is reached through clear speech and the power of expression reaching its depth of meaning as an unutterable background. It is against this background of silent gesture that language proceeds amidst the ceaseless and bewildering course of events that its pure crystal recomposes in countless ways.

Clarity means to make transparent the very foundation of construction, to render its non-constructive foundation evident. Our age is obsessed with the idea of progress, which is meaningful when considering technology that is constructive. But the place of construction in our lives when we consider human flourishing is much more problematic. Psychoanalysis, being a child of its age, inevitably constructed a theoretical edifice to explain mental illness. The concept of progress in this construction was crucial. Psychoanalysis is supposed to be always advancing.

I might say: if the place I want to reach could only be climbed up to by a ladder, I would give up trying to get there. For the place to which I really have to go is one that I must actually be at already.[28]

Progress assumes a solution, an ongoing solution of problems. So it is constructive. We make more and more complicated structures to explain. We start with the clarity of the simple – the supposedly simple 'atoms' out of which something is made; so we reduce things and persons to objects and forces, and from these we make structures that become ever more formalised and complex, an essential productivity.

Philosophy is a battle against the bewitchment of our intelligence by means of language.[29]

The key word here is 'means', which is a translation of *Mittel*, which can also be rendered 'remedy' and 'resources'. It is by calling upon the resources of language that we recover a remedy for our bewitchment. Language is not a mere means. Wittgenstein used the alchemy of the word, for words are potential magic with a power that can transform experience. This can be creative as in literature, but it also has a delusive power.

Direction is sought without the guidance of doctrine. Doubt and despair are essential in finding our way. For the difficulty is not an intellectual one but requires a change of attitude, of restraint of feeling. We must beware of the temptation of soothing explanations, a voice that seeks necessities outside of the conversation, to govern thought and behaviour. The autonomy of discourse and its dialogical character are to be respected. It is this groundlessness that allows subjects to 'be themselves'.

Clarity in therapy would have the same effect as

sunlight on the growth of potato shoots – in a dark cellar they grow long. Clarity could make therapists more aware of the alchemy of the word, and less concerned with the discovery of new methods and theories with their rival claims to truth.

It is not by any means clear to me, that I wish for a continuation of my work by others, more than a change in the way we live, making all these questions superfluous. (For this reason I could never found a school.) [30]

Scepticism

Wittgenstein was a critical thinker. He questioned dogmatic thinking and has been seen by some as belonging to the sceptical tradition in philosophy. [31] But this needs some distinctions, for he was close to the ancient Greek sceptics and not to modern academic scepticism which he frequently criticised. The Greek sceptics were above all therapists, and in some ways their practice of therapy was close to psychoanalysis.

The great strength of ancient Greek scepticism lies in its use of equipollence (*isothenia* – literally, equal force on both sides), that is, a way of setting into opposition equally strong propositions or arguments on both sides of any issue that may arise, and thereby producing an equal balance of justification on both sides of the issue. This may then induce suspension of judgement (*epochē*), which leads to tranquillity and ceasing to dogmatise. This way avoids any essential reliance on beliefs. It does not require reliance on one set of beliefs as a basis for undermining another set and, of course, that includes a 'belief' in scepticism! It does not result in any thesis that is propositional in character.

*If one tried to advance **theses** in philosophy, it would never be possible to debate them, because everyone would agree to them.*[32]

It is not difficult to see that 'suspension of judgement' is not unlike the evenly suspended attention that Freud advocated in the practice of psychoanalysis. He suggested we do not try to ascertain the truth or falsehood of what is said, nor do we try to remember it or note down what seems to be important.[33] Wittgenstein's practice is similar. He does not advance theses or try to increase our beliefs. His task is to resolve the injustices of philosophy, to dissolve the problems like a lump of sugar in water.

The philosopher exaggerates, shouts, as it were, in his helplessness, so long as he hasn't discovered the core of his confusion.[34]

Is this not what we do when in a neurotic confusion?

All that philosophy can do is to destroy idols. And that means not creating a new one – for instance as in 'absence of an idol'.[35]

Freud did, however, create 'idols' in his theory-making that were dependent on the ideology expressed in modern scepticism and which have fed back into the practice of psychoanalysis. Modern scepticism raises problems concerning the legitimacy of proceeding from propositions about one subject matter, which it assumes we know, to another subject matter which it argues is problematic. Thus a common problem is our knowledge of the external world and other people; it is assumed dogmatically that we know our own current mental states but that we cannot justify statements about mind-independent things. Freud assumed that we are essentially atomised individuals, and that reason and knowledge can only be generated out of the resources available to each separated individual. So we have to infer the presence of others and the external world,[36] as well as unconscious states and processes. He thought that the new-born baby and 'primitive' people were like monads shut inside their own minds, only able to relate to others and the world outside by magical thinking.

Wittgenstein showed that human relationships are of a practical and finite nature. They are lived and experienced, and need acknowledgement rather than justification and proof. Freud tried to justify our awareness of the presence of others. When he theorised, he had a purely abstract approach, and so concluded that we can only infer the presence of humans with feelings and thoughts. But our acknowledgement of others is far deeper than theory. It is meaningless to affirm or deny the presence of others in the world, because the concept of *acknowledgement* is deeper than affirmation or negation. Babies acknowledge the presence of other human beings very early in life.

'We see emotion' – As opposed to what? – We do not see facial contortions and make inferences from them (like a doctor framing a diagnosis) to joy, grief, boredom. We describe a face immediately as sad, radiant, bored, even when we are unable to

give any other description of the features. – Grief, one would like to say, is personified in the face. This belongs to the concept of emotion.[37]

The body is expressive of emotion but it is not the bodily movements that are the emotion. We respond to the person, not the body, and he or she is seen in a context and timing that weave into its significance.

Wittgenstein questions sceptical doubts by pointing out sceptical scenarios. He wrote satirically of the sceptic acting out absurd scenes such as turning his attention to his own consciousness.[38] Freud invites us to do this when he claims that 'our acts of consciousness' are immediate data.[39] We start doubting whether others are in pain or not; or wondering whether everything is really in our minds, when we sit in our studies and theorise, cut off from involvement in the world and our natural use of language. We are then tempted to attend inwardly to what we suppose is our certain knowledge of subjective experience. When we do this, our words cease to mean, and we need to be reminded of their everyday use.

Does a child believe that milk exists? Or does it know that milk exists? Does a cat know that a mouse exists?[40]

Scepticism shows us that our primary relation to the world is not through knowledge.

Knowledge

One is often bewitched by a word. For example, by the word 'know'.[41]

Freud was a child of modernity, insisting, despite his practical experience with neurotics, that the accumulation of knowledge is the way to solve our problems. He saw himself as a scientist, and so thought he had increased knowledge with his 'discovery' of the unconscious and the various mental mechanisms causing neurosis. He created a veritable industry producing knowledge of how to cure the various types of human misery. But knowledge is deceptive.

The Oedipus Complex is one of Freud's most famous 'discoveries'. According to him, it plays a fundamental role in the structuring of the personality. On his reading of Sophocles' play *Oedipus Tyrannus*, Oedipus acts out unconscious childhood wishes that we all share – to possess one parent and to kill the other. This fact, according to Freud, accounts for the appeal the play has for us. Unfortunately a closer reading shows that there is no evidence for this.[42]

Freud does not show that Oedipus kills his father and marries his mother *because* he has 'Oedipal wishes'. He produces no evidence that Oedipus is acting out Oedipal phantasies, as opposed to some other.

The play is about the dangers and complexities of 'knowingness'.[43] The name Oedipus in Greek has resonances of 'swollen footed' and 'to know': he is weak-footed but strong-minded. Throughout the play, his 'knowingness' is emphasised. He becomes the tyrant of Thebes because of his cleverness rather than who he is. He solves the riddle of the Sphinx, and she goes and kills herself, but wreaks the terrible vengeance of the plague on Thebes. Oedipus does not kill her himself as the usual hero does.

Oedipus continually jumps to conclusions, as though too anxious to grasp the full meaning of what he is doing. He assumes meaning is transparent to human reason and that he knows what the problem is. He has been told that he will kill his father and marry his mother, yet he quickly kills a man old enough to be his father and marries a woman old enough to be his mother – and is proud of it! On hearing an oracle – notorious for their ambiguity – he immediately assumes he knows what it means.

Sophocles is giving a critique of 'knowingness'. Oedipus was abandoned by his parents and in response abandons himself to 'knowing'. He glorifies the powers of his mind, as it is too painful to recognise his loss. He acts out his abandonment.

Wittgenstein shared many of Sophocles' qualms about knowledge and, like him, sought understanding rather than knowledge. Much of his later writing is a critique of 'knowledge claims' and shows that knowledge is not the basis of our lives.

There are many things we claim to know. For example, I know the 12-times table, who's prime minister and quite a lot about anatomy. In all these cases I can justify my claims by appealing to something independent of me; I could be shown to be wrong. But supposing someone shows me a red spot and I say it is red, and that person then asks: 'How do you know?' One answer is: 'I have learnt English.' But how do I recognise that the spot is red? Have I an image in my mind of red, so when I see red I see that it matches the image? But how do I recognise that my image of red is red? Was I taught this? And how do I know that I have correctly matched my image with the red spot?

When we point to red, we actually point to something red; so we can't determine red just by pointing, for we might be pointing at the shape or surface of the thing that is red.

Reflection on this shows that competence with regard to the basics of one's mother tongue in which one cannot make an error in normal circumstances cannot genuinely be called knowledge.[44] We have to be able to employ words before we can point to things and know them. How do you know how a clarinet sounds; how do you know the taste of coffee; and how do you know what a game is?

*I do not explicitly learn the propositions that stand fast for me. I can **discover** them subsequently like the axis around which a body rotates. This axis is not fixed in the sense that anything holds it fast, but the movement around it determines its immobility.*[45]

There are many things I was not explicitly taught – for example, that my hands don't disappear when I am not paying attention to them, that the earth existed long before I was born and will continue to exist when I am dead, that there are physical objects, that I have a body, that I was born on the earth and not the moon. Our life consists in our being content to accept many things. Knowledge and reason depend on these basics. They are only possible if one trusts something.

In psychosis this trust may be absent. Thus some people do not 'know' if they are alive or dead and may try to prove they are alive by trying to kill themselves. For the ordinary person their being alive is not a question of knowledge. What would you say if you were told you were dead? 'Well, I can move and speak.' But supposing you were told you were an automaton?

'I believe that he is not an automaton', just like that, so far makes no sense. My attitude towards him is an attitude towards a soul. I am not of the **opinion** *that he has a soul.*[46]

We normally treat each other and react to each other differently from the way we treat automata. This is natural and not a matter of belief, hypothesis or knowledge. A baby very early on responds differently to people than to objects. Our actions and utterances, sanity and madness, sense of community, rests upon a trust, a shared form of life. We share common responses – humour, sadness, sense of significance and of fulfilment, what a rebuke, an appeal, a punishment is, what is and is not the case.

This attunement is not anything absolute. Our thinking and understanding are partly determined by a background of ordinary practice. There are bounds to the normal and tolerances that are part of the grammar of human life.

It is always by favour of Nature that one knows something.[47] *Knowledge is in the end based on acknowledgement.*[48]

One of the attractions of psychoanalysis is that it claims to know the inner world, which to many seems a mysterious hidden place. Freud modelled the inner world on the objective physical world as described by what he knew of the physics of his day. He created the picture of some sort of mechanism underlying conscious mental states. However, people do not appear to be mechanisms, we do not treat them as such, but according to Freud they are 'underneath'.

Wittgenstein sought to demystify the inner world in order to bring home inner aliveness.[49] That the inner is hidden seems an undeniable truth. We often do not know what people feel or think. We all can keep our thoughts and feelings to ourselves; in fact, are encouraged to in the teaching of manners.

Furthermore, we may not be sure what we ourselves think or feel about some matters, and we often do things without knowing why. Also, we can misread someone, even when that person is trying hard to make himself or herself understood. And, of course, dreams and slips of the tongue show us that much about our own life is mysterious.

*I think unforeseeability must be **an** essential property of the mental. Just like the endless multiplicity of expression.*[50]

I meet a friend; he smiles and is pleased to see me. How do I know this? If I ask him, how do I know he is not telling lies? The point is, it is not a matter of knowledge here but rather of understanding, for we are playing with flexible concepts that require judgement to understand. We can only say we know when no error is possible or where there are clear rules of evidence. In the weave of ordinary life, we are more concerned with making sense than knowing. This is possible only if we are familiar with the people and have found our feet with them. In a country with entirely strange traditions people could be an enigma even if we knew their language.

Of course, pretence has its outward signs, otherwise we could not talk of it. But a child has to develop before it can pretend. Only when there is a relatively complicated pattern of life do we speak of pretence. When would we first say of a child that he or she is pretending? We must have a sense of genuineness before we can see pretence.

Judgements about the genuineness of expressions of thoughts and feelings require a feel for people and are not a matter of accumulating knowledge.

Can someone else be a man's teacher in this? Certainly. From time to time he gives him the right tip. – This is what 'learning' and 'teaching' are like here. What one acquires here is not a technique; one learns correct judgements.[51]

We have to go by imponderable evidence and this includes subtleties of glance, gesture and tone.

Ask yourself: How does a man learn to get a 'nose' for something? And how can this nose be used?[52]

Unfortunately, psychoanalysts rarely ask this question in their anxiety when faced with the aliveness of the inner. With rare exceptions – for example,

Bion[53] in his later work – they feel compelled to alleviate their anxiety by creating myths of 'knowing'. Is accumulating a knowledge of imagined inner mechanisms the best way to develop 'a nose' for human understanding? Interpretations made as if giving knowledge of the inner world are close to paranoia, for the paranoid person has lost his (or her) feet with people and so is desperate to know. He is endlessly suspicious as he fruitlessly seeks to know the contents of other minds.

One who philosophises often makes the wrong, inappropriate gesture for a verbal expression.[54]

Theory

Freud made certain assumptions in his theory-making that express the ideology of scientism. This is a position that purports to stand outside the sciences and look on them as a whole, assuming that they are the only legitimate form of explanation and truth.[55] Its chief marks are reductionism and determinism. Freud's belief that all mental events are determined was such that in his presence students had to give explanations for everything they did, such as why one did not hold one's spoon in the proper way or why one did such-and-such a thing in such-and-such a manner.[56] Wittgenstein suggested that this is closer to superstition than reason. Why *must* there be an explanation for everything?

The development of science actually suggests that science is a family-relation concept of various human practices seeking knowledge, which have some features in common, but no set is definitive for all. Contrast mathematical physics with palaeontology.

Misleading parallel: psychology treats of processes in the psychical sphere, as does physics in the physical.[57]

Most Freudian theory is based on this misleading parallel. It enables theorists to reduce the activities of people to processes in their minds. It assumes that there are psychical objects, events and mental processes in the psychical domain similar to physical objects in the physical one. Consciousness *makes each of us aware only of his own states of mind.*[58] These states are reported to the psychologist and, like the physicist, his job is to discover the 'real state' of things, which are abstract objects and processes deep in the unconscious.

Wittgenstein wanted to change this way of seeing

and conceptualising people. He replaced theory by carefully describing how we are initiated into language and how it is used.

We want to replace wild conjectures and explanations by quiet weighing of linguistic facts.[59]

He resisted the compulsion 'to penetrate phenomena' to seek some ultimate cause.[60] He did not seek anything hidden, because everything already 'lies open to view'. Things appear hidden, not because they are below the surface, rather because they are familiar and simple and always before our eyes.[61] It is the idealising gaze that compels us to look for mysterious entities, whereas we need to see what actually *is*.

It is not by inspecting our own images, feelings and thoughts that we understand what they are. They are not apart from language; we have to see how the concepts are used to make sense of them.

What is most difficult here is to put this indefiniteness, correctly and unfalsified, into words.[62]

Although Freud described idealisation as a defence against a loved object,[63] psychoanalysts idealise in their theorising – for example, the idea of a 'mind' or an 'unconscious' as some sort of ghostly entities is an idealisation.

One of the most dangerous of ideas for a philosopher is, oddly enough, that we think with our heads or in our heads. The idea of thinking as a process in the head, in a completely enclosed space, gives him something occult.[64]

Wittgenstein pointed out that we can characteristically calculate 'in our heads'. Calculating in the head appears to be something that essentially goes on inwardly, 'in our mind', so it seems it can be clarified by attending to what happens inwardly. But we first have to be able to calculate on paper or out loud before we can grasp what calculating in the head is. It is a misconception that what is 'inner' is a mental process that makes sense by inwardly observing it.[65]

Despite his remarkable sensibility, when he theorised Freud returned again and again to the refuge of thinking in his head. But when we make gestures of love or deep grief, we gesture towards our hearts, not our heads, for love and grief are not processes in our minds. The picture of thought in the head has become embedded in psychoanalysis and characterises its theorising.

How do we compare the behaviour of anger, joy, hope, expectation, belief, love and understanding? – Act like an angry person! That's easy. Like a joyful one – here it would depend on what the joy was about. The joy of seeing someone again, or the joy of listening to a piece of music . . . ? – Hope? That would be hard. Why? There are no gestures of hope.[66]

The finer features of behaviour provide the criteria in which the inner is characterised. Thus love is often thought to be a unique feeling, a brute given, which we cannot fail to identify – after all we feel it 'inside' ourselves. But love is not to be characterised in this way. It is put to the test; to feel love for an hour or two is infatuation. The grammar of love is not that of an intense feeling; how we understand it reflects much else in our lives.

What we see in psychology, as in ordinary life, is the expressive behaviour of the subject; his (or her) manifestations of thought, belief and desire. His utterances give expression to experiences, they do not report them and neither are they mere signs of

mental processes that go on inside the subject. If we
are sad we express our sadness. It is 'on' our faces
and 'in' our gestures. It is 'real'. It is not in our
minds and so does not involve observing them and
reporting any mental processes going on inside
them. The psychologist observes the phenomena *of*
seeing, believing, thinking, wishing, for our words
are an expression of our lives.[67]

*Our language can be seen as an ancient city: a maze
of little streets and squares, of old and new houses,
and of houses with additions from various periods;
and this surrounded by a multitude of new boroughs
with straight regular streets and uniform houses.*[68]

Logic and grammar appear everywhere. The straight
roads and uniform houses are scientific theories and
much mathematics. Factual assertions, emotions
and feelings, intention, sensation and gesture are in
the centre where we spend most of our lives.

Ordinary talk in therapy is mostly in the language
of the ancient city. Psychoanalysis rests on theory
and so has a technical language which now requires
special dictionaries. It seeks to replace ordinary
language, which has grown out of the needs and
practices of everyday life. But by applying theory to

therapy we place a pre-conceived hypothesis forward against which a person and his or her actions are evaluated and explained. A good theory is neat, with straight regular streets. It is useful when used as a measuring rod, an object of comparison, to help people look at their problems in a fresh light. But when it becomes dogmatic, something to which reality must correspond, then it can lead to new problems. We become bewitched by theory and idealise it, then we interpret according to the theory. It becomes like a spectacle lens through which we see things with the distortion produced by the lens.

This generalising impulse fuelling theory is prevalent in psychoanalysis. Freud was a master at finding good stories to explain: all dreams are wish fulfilment, we primarily desire pleasure, all mankind suffers from the Oedipus Complex and so on.

Anyone who listens to a child's crying with understanding will know that psychic forces, terrible forces, sleep within it, different from anything commonly assumed. Profound rage & pain & lust for destruction.[69]

The cry shows but cannot say because it has no grammar. We cannot say that the child fears annihilation or persecution because it does not have these concepts. Our original language-learning involves coming to understand what language shows without explicit instruction. This is a natural human capacity. Training creates the stable structure in terms of which meaning comes into view. Meaning cannot be explained until we have acquired a fairly sophisticated use of language.

How is the connection between words and sensations set up? We need to describe how the child learns this. A child does not need to be taught to cry, nor need the child 'cry for a reason'. The infant is not able to interpret or understand his (or her) own behaviour. But his behaviour will have meaning for his care-takers. So if he falls down and cries they may comfort it and say things like: 'Never mind; you will be all right', 'Up you get' and so on. As Wittgenstein put it:

Words are connected with the primitive, the natural, expressions of the sensation and are used in its place.[70]

Eventually the verbal expression of pain replaces crying and does not describe it. So the outer expression provides the criteria in terms of which the inner is characterised. The child learns to represent pain to itself and use the concept of pain in multiple ways. It thereby gains access to the logical space necessary for more sophisticated concepts such as hope or intention.

Instead of postulating two minds – a conscious one and an unconscious hidden behind it with its tacit rules – we can say that the child moves from preconceptual or archaic thinking to conceptual thinking, which enables it to speak in accordance with the rules of grammar appropriate to its way of life with others.

So we can understand Freud's practice without having to adopt his models of the mind. Take the question of little Hans' 'widdler'. Little Hans, aged five, had a phobia that horses would bite him and he was cured of this by Freud.[71] Now little Hans took a lively interest in his own 'widdler' and he thought that both his parents had one, as had his little sister, and that a cow's udder was one. Freud assumed that by 'widdler' little Hans meant penis and that little Hans, like all children, was a little scientist trying to discover facts about sex and that he merely misinterpreted his observational data rather than abandon his theory.

But on what grounds?[72] Little Hans was correct about his own widdler and about the penises of animals at the zoo. However, he thought a cow's udder is one; he also thought that if his own 'widdler' were ever to be cut off he would widdle with his bottom. Could little Hans have concepts that demarcate objects? Could he point to penises and say, 'That is one'? Clearly he could not.

It is not clear what he would have called things like an elephant's trunk or an anteater's nose. There is simply a family resemblance between these various 'widdlers'. He was in no position to develop theories that require a sophisticated background of language and the ability to conceptualise.

Little Hans could not think, his 'thought' was archaic. He could only wish – that is, produce imagistic representations of the conditions that would satisfy it, as in dreaming. His associations to him were not loose, they were only loose to those who judged at an adult level. As far as he was concerned, it is not a mistake to call an udder a widdler. The meaning of 'widdler' must be given by what he does and would call a widdler, not by some image in his mind. His loose associations represent the child's archaic sense of similarity, difference and relevance.

Little Hans had not developed the concept of a penis. Under emotional pressure, as after a trauma, he felt anxiety. Anxiety, however, is not about something determinate: it lacks an object and is felt as a tension, it is at the limit of language. Freud's interpretations helped to complete a process of mental development. He recognised the family resemblances among the loose associations of the archaic mind and his interpretations enabled little Hans to develop the concept of a penis. Then he could express and instantiate the concept and move from anxiety to fear. This has a determinate object and so is meaningful and can be desired or avoided. His mental development could resume and his wishes could develop into desires.

Archaic thought continues into adult life and may disrupt it. But we need not follow Freud's explanations. Thus a fetish, which Freud thought was a substitute for the mother's penis and was a triumph over the threat of castration,[73] is better understood as having an archaic meaning and involved in wishing. The fetishist is wishing for a 'penis', but is not desiring a penis, nor fearful of castration, in the adult sense.

Causes and Reasons

It was reported that Wittgenstein thought that the confusion of reason and cause had led the followers of Freud into an 'abominable mess'.[74] Freud believed in psychical determinism; he believed that unconscious processes really take place and so constitute the determining cause and contain the real meaning of the action to be explained.

If an event A is the cause of an event B, then one would need to verify, in a sufficient number of cases, that A is regularly followed by B. Causes are established by experiment, through statistics or by seeing a mechanism, such as when we see one billiard ball hit another, thus causing the second ball to move.

Reasons are established differently. They are justifications for action, so the person who acts is usually the authority. 'Why did you get up from your chair?' 'To make a cup of tea.' That is the reason. But there could be other reasons according to circumstances – for example, 'To hit you', 'Because I heard the fire alarm', 'Because I feel anxious if I sit for long' and so on. We do not look inside ourselves and report the reason, for there is no independent means of access to it, so there can be no question of reporting correctly or not. It is part of the grammar of reason that the agent should know it, for our interest is in the agent's own account of his or her action. Their grammar is linked to that of motives, desires and intention.

A reason is a good one if it corresponds to a certain standard of a good reason, and this is partly a matter of culture, discussion and agreement. In some cultures men beat their wives because they love them. This would not be seen as a good reason in Western culture, but this does not mean it is a bad one in others.

Reasons are expressions of the person's inner life and so we depend on truthfulness and sincerity in assessing them. When a person acts, we assume he is acting with intent and if asked can tell us why. This goes with the assumption that the act is voluntary. Reasons take place on the same dimension as the action itself, for reasons can precede action. I want to make a cup of tea, so I get up from my chair. Reasons run out; I can give no further reason why I acted as I did. Causes, on the other hand, form an infinite chain and do not capture the notion of decision and choice, both of which are central to our understanding of ourselves and others.

Of course, we can be confused about our reasons. We can deceive ourselves and others, and other people may be more perceptive about our reasons than we are; but these abilities only make sense against a background of sincerity. If all reasons were insincere, the notion of reason would collapse.

The confusion of reasons and causes leads to the belief that the certainties of scientific knowledge have been extended to reason. It gives a false certainty to psychoanalysis, so its claims appear unarguable. We cannot argue with an expert on causes, but we can with someone who tells us of a reason for our action that does not make sense to us.

Ritual

Both Freud and Wittgenstein were interested in ritual and myth, but understood them very differently. Freud thought science was a superior form of knowledge, so he judged ritual and myth in terms of error. He was extraordinarily chauvinistic, believing that we see in Western culture the fullest flowering of the human spirit and the *telos* towards which 'less advanced civilisations' will eventually, if belatedly, make their hapless way. He assumed myths were primitive scientific theories. As he lived in an age in which everything is to be explained and evaluated for its utility, he subjected myth and ritual to these processes. Wittgenstein was careful only to describe and do justice to the facts, avoiding explanations based on contemporary beliefs that there is a universal human nature.

In order to marvel human beings – and perhaps peoples – have to wake up. Science is a way of sending them off to sleep again.[75]

'Primitive' people and children can marvel at things around them, whereas it is difficult for us to do so; and if we do, then scientists and psychoanalysts are ready to step in and explain why we do not need to.

Formality is a characteristic feature of human beings. Nearly all social action is to some degree formalised. All cultures have prescribed forms of good manners; corporate actions have formalities such as the various ways to call and hold meetings, there are formalities around birth, marriage and death, and the variety of descent systems are formalised. All 'animal' activities such as copulation, excretion, hunting and eating are governed by rules and symbolic usages. Language has a formal structure in its sounds and grammar. The way we speak and when to speak is formalised, as are different forms of writing – news, essays, novels, poetry, scientific papers.

Ritual is an expression in social action of formality and so has symbolic features. It is not dependent on opinion. People taking part in it may have opinions on what it means, but these opinions are often ritualised. There are no real reasons for most ritual acts. The pure pointlessness of some customs is part of their nature. It gives a depth to them, a sense of wonder. An inner attitude such as grief or rejoicing, may be given expression through formal behaviour. But the same attitude can be comprehensively expressed through very different forms of conduct. Thus funeral ceremonies vary enormously across different cultures: singing and dancing, even eating the dead body, can be just as respectful as long faces and tears.

Explanations are out of place. Genetic explanations, such as appeal to the laws of evolution, human development and historical reconstruction, have a limited use, as the significance of a rite does not reside solely in its development. Some rituals have a clear beginning – for example, the Eucharist – but most do not. The expressions 'Long, long ago' and 'Once upon a time' are evocative and to the point. Rituals do not necessarily have a clear meaning. Participants usually give disparate meanings or just say: 'It is the thing to do', 'We have always done it this way' and so on. This is neither rational nor irrational, for ritual is self-sustaining and self-justifying since man is a ceremonial animal.

Radically different ways of life will give birth to

rituals that we find difficult to understand. Many peoples have thought that courage and honour are more important than the length of one's life. At the birth of a boy, the Aztec midwife would chant a song wishing the child: 'Death by the obsidian knife' – that is, the child, if fortunate, would, in his early 20s, die a warrior's death in combat or on the killing stone in an enemy city. The Aztec parents were noted by the Spaniards for being very tender and loving to their children.

It is a great temptation to make the spirit explicit.[76]

The simplicity or symmetry of an explanation can be a charm, which helps to understand the popularity of Freudian and Jungian explanations. But a closer look shows that there is no unified account of ritual. To theorise it is to be blind to its meaning. It can serve many purposes – expressing emotion, creating meaning and belief, a cement to keep a group together, a drama, a way of empowering and constraining certain people, a form of therapy, a way of passing on cultural knowledge. It is an essential part of the natural history of human beings and of the day-to-day practice of psychoanalysis, and it can give us access to our own nature.

The Self

What is good and evil is essentially the I, not the world.

The I, the I is what is deeply mysterious![77]

Freud and Wittgenstein were both deeply concerned to understand 'the self' and there is a huge literature in psychoanalysis on this. But the two men characteristically approached it in very different ways.

Psychoanalysts produce theories of the 'self' that are varied and often complicated. As theories they objectify, and try to describe and explain what is going on 'in' the mind. They create entities, such as ego and self, and describe what they do and the relations between them. For psychoanalysis, identification is the operation whereby the human subject is constituted. The little boy's identification with his father, the identification that occurs in groups, identification with the aggressor, the ego ideal and identification with one's gender are all examples. The ego is understood as an agency and as the product of identifications.

These are all theories and make no difference to how analysts live their lives. There is no empirical evidence that holders of one theory help more people than those of an opposing one, although psychoanalysis is supposed to be an empirical science.

Wittgenstein attended to how we use 'I' rather than discussing theoretical entities. There are about eight occurrences of 'I' per page of *Philosophical Investigations* and about four of 'we'.[78] Few philosophical texts have anything like that number. He is showing how he falls under the spell of various pictures embedded in language, and his struggle to free himself. He was careful not to develop a positive account of the self; he did not seek to reappropriate a 'self'.[79] One may know what he says but still be deeply confused about oneself.

Some of his thought can be summed up as pointing out that 'I' does not refer to, or name, any entity; 'I' is not 'me'.[80] Thinking takes place but is not done by an agent locked in the mind, although we mostly act and think as though it were. Supposing I say that I have failed a number of things. Grammatically I am stating a number of facts, expressing my upset, and saying 'I' spontaneously, which is very different from stating that I am a failure – meaning 'I' equals failure. This is to imagine that 'I' refers to some entity that I imagine is inside me. One becomes a slave to one's imaginings. Similarly if I think that I am a success. It could be factually so – for example,

I am Chair of an important company. But it may 'go to my head' and I think 'I' equals success. Instead of expressing my delight, I think 'in my head' that success is a property of 'I'. This may lead to my becoming manic, conceited and so on, and losing the spontaneity of 'I'.

'I' is often thought to equal one's 'real self', one's identity, and this is connected to being recognised for who one is. What do we mean by identity? There are many ways of identifying a person – his or her appearance, history, name, fingerprint, DNA, identity card and so on. But all these seem to leave out who I 'really' am. Is there an inner essence, the real me, which has continued up to now and resides behind all the outward qualities?[81] Do only I know who I really am? How do I find out? After all, in amnesia a person may say: 'I don't know who I am', meaning they have forgotten their name, where they live and so on. Some people may continually feel and say: 'I am dead', or 'I don't exist'. But note they all correctly say 'I'.

There is no one thing that constitutes my identity. 'I' am not an entity with a set of properties. The demand for identity and the criteria for it vary according to the context. When we feel recognised, what is important is the spontaneous response by the other, their familiarity with us rather than the correct identification of particular traits or of some essence – the real me. Identification is the wheel that binds us to neurotic suffering. The meaning of 'I' is surrounded by dense mists of language, so it is almost impossible to think clearly and see 'I' is not me. But showing differences is central to Wittgenstein's therapy.

'I feel great joy.' – Where? – That sounds like non-sense. And yet one does say 'I feel a joyful agitation in my breast'. – But why is joy not localised? Is it because it is distributed over the whole body? Even where the feeling that arouses joy is not localised, joy is not: if for example we rejoice in the smell of a flower. – Joy is manifested in facial expression, in behaviour. (But we do not say we are joyful in our faces.)

'But I do have a real feeling of joy!' Yes, when you are glad you really are glad . . .

'But "joy" surely designates an inward thing.' No. 'Joy' designates nothing at all. Neither any inward nor any outward thing.[82]

Where and what is the self? It is not a stable unity and has no substance in joy.

Such and much more such the hubbub in his mind so-called till nothing left from deep within but only ever fainter oh to end. No matter how no matter where. Time and grief and self so-called. Oh all to end.[83]

Notes

1. N. Malcolm, *Ludwig Wittgenstein: A Memoir*, 2nd edition, Oxford University Press, 1984, p. 101.

2. RFM 2, para 23.

3. C&V, p. 25.

4. C&V, p. 41.

5. C&V, p. 4.

6. C&V, p. 28.

7. C&V, p. 44.

8. PO, p. 165.

9. S. Freud, *Introductory Lectures on Psychoanalysis* (1916–17), Penguin, 1973.

10. C&V, p. 64.

11. C&V, p. 86.

12. PI, p. 223.

13. C&V, p. 50.

14. PI, p. 220.

15. PR 3, para 27.

16. Z, para 382.

17. PO, p. 107.

18. PI, p. 193.

19. PO, p. 163.

20. PI, para 115.

21. L&C, pp. 45–48.

22. C&V, p. 24.

23. TLP, pp. 19–25 (4-4.0621).

24. PI, paras 527–29.

25. D. W. Winnicott, *Therapeutic Consultations in Child Psychiatry*, London: Hogarth Press, 1971.

26. N. Bryson, *Vision and Painting: The Logic of the Gaze,* London: Macmillan, 1983, pp. 87–131.

27. C&V, p. 23.

28. C&V, p. 10.

29. PI, para 109.

30. C&V, p. 70.

31. R. J. Fogelin, *Wittgenstein*, 2nd edition, London: Routledge and Kegan Paul, 1987, pp. 226–34.

32. PI, para 128.

33. S. Freud, *Recommendations to Physicians Practising Psycho-analysis* (1912), S.E. 12:109–20.

34. PO, p. 181.

35. PO, p. 171.

36. S. Freud, 'The Unconscious' (1915) in *On Metapsychology: The Theory of Psychoanalysis*, Penguin, 1984, p. 170.

37. Z, para 225.

38. PI, para 412.

39. S. Freud, 'An Outline of Psychoanalysis' (1940) in *Historical and Expository Works on Psychoanalysis*, Penguin, 1993, p. 376.

40. OC, para 478.

41. OC, para 435.

42. J. Lear, *Open Minded*, Cambridge, Mass.: Harvard

University Press, 1998, pp. 33–55.

43. J-J. Goux, *Oedipus, Philosopher*, trans. C. Porter, Stanford University Press, 1993.

44. OC, paras 526–31.

45. OC, para 152.

46. PI, p. 178.

47. OC, para 505.

48. OC, para 378.

49. H.L. Finch, *Wittgenstein*, Rockport, Mass.: Element Books, 1995, pp. 73–90.

50. LW2, p. 65.

51. PI, p. 227.

52. PI, p. 228.

53. W.R. Bion, *Attention and Interpretation*, London: Tavistock, 1970.

54. Z, para 450.

55. J. Bouveresse, *Wittgenstein Reads Freud: The Myth of the Unconscious*, trans. C. Cosman, New Jersey: Princeton University Press, 1995.

56. Ibid., p. 91.

57. PI, para 571.

58. S. Freud, 'The Unconscious' (1915) in *On Metapsychology: The Theory of Psychoanalysis*, Penguin, 1984, p. 170.

59. Z, para 447.

60. PI, para 90.

61. PI, para 129.

62. PI, p. 227.

63. S. Freud, 'On Narcissism' (1914) in *On Metapsychology: The Theory of Psychoanalysis*, Penguin, 1984, p. 65.

64. Z, paras 605–6.

65. PI, pp. 216, 220.

66. LW1, para 357.

67. Z, para 471.

68. PI, para 18.

69. C&V, p. 4.

70. PI, para 244.

71. S. Freud, 'Analysis of a Phobia in a Five Year Old Boy', Little Hans (1909) in *Case Histories 1*, Penguin, 1977, p. 169.

72. J. Lear, *Love and its Place in Nature*, New Haven and London: Yale University Press, 1998, pp. 98–119.

73. S. Freud, 'Fetishism' (1927), in *On Sexuality*, Penguin, 1977.

74. PO, p. 107.

75. C&V, p. 7.

76. C&V, p. 11.

77. NB, p. 80.

78. J.F. Peterman, *Philosophy as Therapy*, State University of New York Press, 1992, pp. 45–47.

79. H. Sluga, '"Whose house is that?" Wittgenstein on the Self' in H. Sluga and D.G. Stern (eds.), *The Cambridge Companion to Wittgenstein*, Cambridge

University Press, 1996.
80. PI, paras 398–411.
81. PI, paras 390–411.
82. Z, paras 486–87.
83. S. Beckett, 'Stirrings Still' in *As the Story was Told*, London: John Calder Riverrun Press, 1990, p. 128.

Bibliography

Wittgenstein's *Philosophical Investigations*, edited by G.E.M. Anscombe and R. Rhees, and translated by G.E.M. Anscombe (Oxford: Blackwell) is the main source of his thoughts on psychology and therapy. A good commentary is *Wittgenstein and the Philosophical Investigations* by M. McGinn (London: Routledge, 1997). Other sources are included in the notes.

There are many books on Wittgenstein. Those relevant to therapy and postmodernism include the following.

Freud and Wittgenstein, B. McGuinness, in 'Wittgenstein and his Times', ed. B. McGuinness, Oxford: Blackwell, 1982.

Freudian Repression, M. Billig, Cambridge University Press, 1999.

Insight and Illusion, 2nd edition, P.M.S. Hacker, Oxford: Clarendon Press, 1986.

Love and its Place in Nature, J. Lear, New Haven and London: Yale University Press, 1998.

The Danger of Words and Writings on Wittgenstein, M.O'C. Drury, Bristol: Thoemmes Press, 1996.

Wittgenstein and Derrida, H. Staten, Oxford: Blackwell, 1985.

Wittgenstein on Freud and Fraser, F. Cioffi, Cambridge University Press, 1998.

WITTGENSTEIN AND PSYCHOANALYSIS

Wittgenstein on Mind and Language, D. G. Stern, Oxford University Press, 1995.

Wittgenstein Reads Freud: The Myth of the Unconscious, trans. C. Cosman, J. Bouveresse, New Jersey: Princeton University Press, 1995.

Wittgenstein's Art of Investigation, B. Savickey, London and New York: Routledge, 1999.

Abbreviations

References to Wittgenstein's works come from the following publications.

C&V   *Culture and Value*, revised 2nd edition, ed. G.H. von Wright, trans. P. Winch, Blackwell, 1998.

L&C   *Lectures and Conversations on Aesthetics, Psychology and Religious Belief*, ed. C. Barrett, Blackwell, 1966.

LW1   *Last Writings on the Philosophy of Psychology*, vol. 1, trans. C.G. Luckhardt and M.A.E. Aue, Blackwell, 1982.

LW2   *Last Writings on the Philosophy of Psychology*, vol. 2, trans. C.G. Luckhardt and M.A.E. Aue, Blackwell, 1992.

NB   *Notebooks: 1914–16*, 2nd edition, trans. G.E.M. Anscombe, Blackwell, 1979.

OC   *On Certainty*, trans. D. Paul and G.E.M. Anscombe, Blackwell, 1979.

PI   *Philosophical Investigations*, trans. G.E.M. Anscombe, Blackwell, 1958.

PO   *Philosophical Occasions 1912–1951*, ed. J.C. Klagge and A. Nordmann, Hackett Publications, 1993.

PR   *Philosophical Remarks*, trans. R. Hargreaves and R. White, Blackwell, 1975.

RFM   *Remarks on the Foundations of Mathematics*, trans. G. E. M. Anscombe, Blackwell, 1978.

RPP1   *Remarks on the Philosophy of Psychology*, vol. 1, trans. G. E. M. Anscombe, Blackwell, 1980.

TLP   *Tractatus Logico-Philosophicus*, trans. D. F. Pears and B. F. McGuinness, Routledge and Kegan Paul, 1961.

Z   *Zettel*, trans. G. E. M. Anscombe, 2nd edition, Blackwell, 1981.

Acknowledgements

The author gratefully acknowledges Blackwell Publishers for permission to reprint extracts from Wittgenstein's writing. The extract from N. Malcolm, *Ludwig Wittgenstein: A Memoir* (1984) is reprinted by permission of Oxford University Press.

Other titles available in the Postmodern Encounters series from Icon/Totem

Derrida and the End of History
Stuart Sim

ISBN 1 84046 094 6
UK £2.99   USA $7.95

What does it mean to proclaim 'the end of history', as several thinkers have done in recent years? Francis Fukuyama, the American political theorist, created a considerable stir in *The End of History and the Last Man* (1992) by claiming that the fall of communism and the triumph of free market liberalism brought an 'end of history' as we know it. Prominent among his critics has been the French philosopher Jacques Derrida, whose *Specters of Marx* (1993) deconstructed the concept of 'the end of history' as an ideological confidence trick, in an effort to salvage the unfinished and ongoing project of democracy.

Derrida and the End of History places Derrida's claim within the context of a wider tradition of 'endist' thought. Derrida's critique of endism is highlighted as one of his most valuable contributions to the postmodern cultural debate – as well as being the most accessible entry to *deconstruction*, the controversial philosophical movement founded by him.

Stuart Sim is Professor of English Studies at the University of Sunderland. The author of several works on critical and cultural theory, he edited *The Icon Critical Dictionary of Postmodern Thought* (1998).

Foucault and Queer Theory
Tamsin Spargo
ISBN 1 84046 092 X
UK £2.99   USA $7.95

Michel Foucault is the most gossiped-about celebrity of
French poststructuralist theory. The homophobic insult
'queer' is now proudly reclaimed by some who once
called themselves lesbian or gay. What is the connection
between the two?

This is a postmodern encounter between Foucault's
theories of sexuality, power and discourse and the
current key exponents of queer thinking who have
adopted, revised and criticised Foucault. Our
understanding of gender, identity, sexuality and cultural
politics will be radically altered in this meeting of
transgressive figures.

Foucault and Queer Theory excels as a brief introduction
to Foucault's compelling ideas and the development of
queer culture with its own outspoken views on
heteronormativity, sado-masochism, performativity,
transgender, the end of gender, liberation-versus-
difference, late capitalism and the impact of AIDS on
theories and practices.

Tamsin Spargo worked as an actor before taking up her
current position as Senior Lecturer in Literary and
Historical Studies at Liverpool John Moores University.
She writes on religious writing, critical and cultural
theory and desire.

Nietzsche and Postmodernism
Dave Robinson
ISBN 1 84046 093 8
UK £2.99   USA $7.95

Friedrich Nietzsche (1844–1900) has exerted a huge
influence on 20th century philosophy and literature – an
influence that looks set to continue into the 21st century.
Nietzsche questioned what it means for us to live in our
modern world. He was an 'anti-philosopher' who
expressed grave reservations about the reliability and
extent of human knowledge. His radical scepticism
disturbs our deepest-held beliefs and values. For these
reasons, Nietzsche casts a 'long shadow' on the complex
cultural and philosophical phenomenon we now call
'postmodernism'.

Nietzsche and Postmodernism explains the key ideas of
this 'Anti-Christ' philosopher. It then provides a clear
account of the central themes of postmodernist thought
exemplified by such thinkers as Derrida, Foucault,
Lyotard and Rorty, and concludes by asking if Nietzsche
can justifiably be called the first great postmodernist.

Dave Robinson has taught philosophy for many years. He
is the author of Icon/Totem's introductory guides to
Philosophy, Ethics and Descartes. He thinks that
Nietzsche is a postmodernist, but he's not sure.

Baudrillard and the Millennium
Christopher Horrocks
ISBN 1 84046 091 1
UK £2.99   USA $7.95

'In a sense, we do not believe in the Year 2000', says
French thinker Jean Baudrillard. Still more disturbing
is his claim that the millennium might not take place.
Baudrillard's analysis of 'Y2K' reveals a repentant
culture intent on storing, mourning and laundering its
past, and a world from which even the possibility of the
'end of history' has vanished. Yet behind this bleak vision
of integrated reality, Baudrillard identifies enigmatic
possibilities and perhaps a final ironic twist.

Baudrillard and the Millennium confronts the strategies
of this major cultural analyst's encounter with the
greatest non-event of the postmodern age, and accounts
for the critical censure of Baudrillard's enterprise. Key
topics, such as natural catastrophes, the body, 'victim
culture', identity and Internet viruses, are discussed in
reference to the development of Jean Baudrillard's
millenarian thought from the 1980s to the threshold of
the Year 2000 – from simulation to disappearance.

Christopher Horrocks is Senior Lecturer in Art History
at Kingston University in Surrey. His publications
include *Introducing Baudrillard* and *Introducing Foucault*,
both published by Icon/Totem. He lives in Tulse Hill, in
the south of London.